AN ANCIENT
ROMAN
FORT

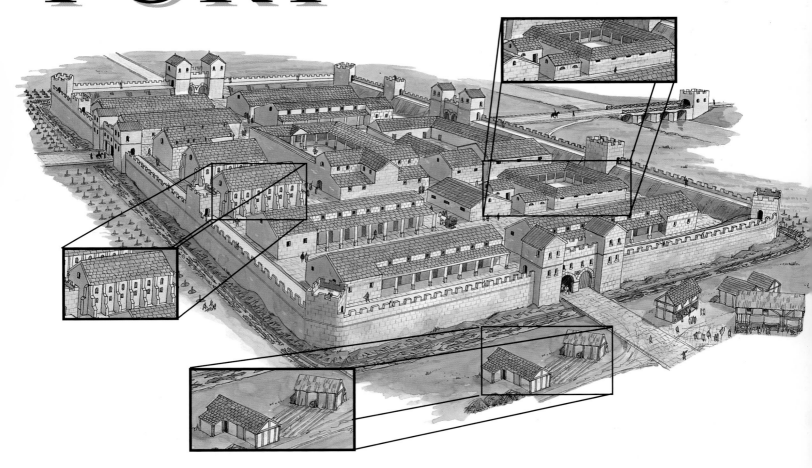

Written by
Stephen Johnson

Illustrated by
Mark Bergin

Series created by
David Salariya

BOOK | HOUSE

Rome

Roman control of such a massive part of the known world had been growing for around 300 years before Hadrian's reign and during that time Rome grew from being just one of many Italian towns into a major world power.

THE ROMAN EMPIRE

IN THE REIGN of the Emperor Hadrian, the Roman Empire circled the whole of the Mediterranean Sea and covered large areas of Europe, the near East and Africa. For those lands inside the Empire, it provided a stable and peaceful society, opportunities for trading goods of many kinds and, above all, security from attack because of its strong and permanent army. In the northern parts of Europe and towards Persia and Iran, the Empire faced real threats to its borders from hostile tribes or other kingdoms. In Africa, there were nomadic tribes who occasionally raided across the border. Troops were based in forts around the frontiers of the Empire to deal with hostile attacks. In some areas, the frontiers took different forms: a wall defended with forts was erected in Britain (Hadrian's Wall); rivers or wooden palisades were used in mainland Europe and in the near East, the frontier was a desert road watched over by a series of towers and small forts.

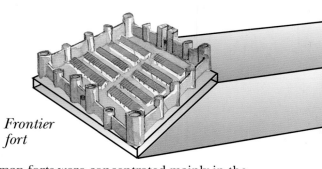

Frontier fort

Roman forts were concentrated mainly in the frontier zones of the Empire. They differed slightly in shape and style, but their layout and buildings were more or less the same.

Captured tribes from conquered nations were encouraged to live like Romans and even join the Roman army. Most of Rome's frontier troops were recruited locally and may once have been those fighting against Rome!

Captured tribesmen

Map of the Roman Empire at its greatest size

Roman frontier

Londinium

GERMANIA

GAUL

DACIA

ITALY

Rome

GREECE

HISPANIA

Carthage

CRETE

Roman frontier

AFRICA

EGYPT

Baggage wagon · Auxiliary archers · Foot soldiers · Standard · Auxiliary centurion

The baggage wagons, carrying equipment and supplies, brought up the rear.

The auxiliaries and officers on horseback were led by the standard bearers and the auxiliary centurion.

Joining the army could make for a good career, but men had to sign on for 25 years' service.

Training was hard – learning to fight the Roman way, working alongside colleagues and using weapons correctly.

When a unit of new recruits was posted abroad the only way to get there was to march, carrying all their equipment.

In a real battle, prisoners were captured and sent back to Rome to become slaves.

THE ROMAN ARMY

MANY DIFFERENT types of troop units made up the Roman army. The key troops were the legions. By the time of Hadrian (AD 117-138) there were around 30 legions stationed in permanent fortresses close to the frontiers of the Roman Empire, totalling more than 150,000 full time legionary soldiers in service. Alongside the legionaries were the auxiliary troops, units added to the army by Rome to bring a range of different fighting techniques from locally recruited soldiers around the Empire. These were foot-soldiers, cavalry or they might have had specialist skills and weapons not normally used by the legions, e.g. archers with bows and arrows or stone throwers using slings.

There were around 500 men in a normal auxiliary cohort. An infantry unit was divided into six centuries, each containing around 80 men (not 100 as the word 'century' implies). A legion of 5-6,000 men was divided into 10 cohorts. Six centuries made up each cohort, commanded by an officer called a tribune. The first cohort in every legion contained its best troops and most senior officers.

Auxiliary soldier

1 Iron helmet covered in bronze
2 Spear
3 Chain mail tunic
4 Sword, similar to legionary equipment
5 Shield, bearing emblems of the unit
6 Woollen trousers
7 Leather sandals

Legionary soldiers
and centurion

Legionary
commander

Next in line was the centurion leading the century under his command.

In front of the legionary centurion were the legion's standards and the commander's bodyguards. The legionary commander was in front.

Troop units were sent on duties all over the Roman Empire and this included sailing to Britain, a wild and cold place!

Broad sword and scabbard

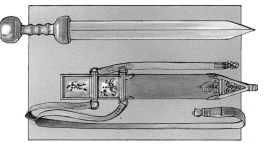

There was a great variety of weapons in the Roman army, but the most important was the broad sword (called the *gladius*). It was quite short and straight and made of sharpened steel. It was very effective, when used by soldiers in tight formation together, to stab and jab at opponents.

The two figures on these pages are an auxiliary soldier (left) and a legionary (right). Auxiliary soldiers were lightly armed and their main protection was chain mail which covered much of their bodies. Auxiliary units often carried special weapons, such as slings (for throwing stones) or bows and arrows. In a battle they provided support for the legionary troops.

The legionaries wore heavier armour of steel plates sewn onto a leather jacket. Their shields were rectangular and curved and could fit together to protect a line of troops advancing in battle. They carried a sword and a dagger, both of which were deadly at close quarters. The throwing spear was weighted so that the point would drive into an enemy. This legionary is shown with his equipment for a march.

Legionary soldier

1 Helmet with neck protector
2 Spear or javelin
3 Body armour of metal plates held together with leather straps
4 Kit bag
5 Cooking pan
6 Digging tool (*dolabra*)
7 Legionary sword with bone handle
8 Dagger
9 Woollen tunic under the armour
10 Shield
11 Sandals

When Roman ships docked in northern Britain it was still a long march for soldiers posted to the frontier wall being built on Hadrian's orders.

On arrival, soldiers had to help build the fort in which they would live.

The Roman army was also responsible for building the roads connecting the forts along Hadrian's Wall.

9

Choice of site was important. A fort needed good views in all directions and a source of fresh water not too far away.

Clearing the wood and undergrowth from the chosen site was the first step. Wood was used for the first defences, gates and buildings.

Surveyors used a device called a *groma* to plan the layout of the fort and ensure the buildings, roads, gates and ditches were in the right places.

Once a fort became permanent, its early wooden buildings were replaced in stone.

Earth from the narrow, V-shaped fort ditches was piled up to form a wide rampart bank to give added protection.

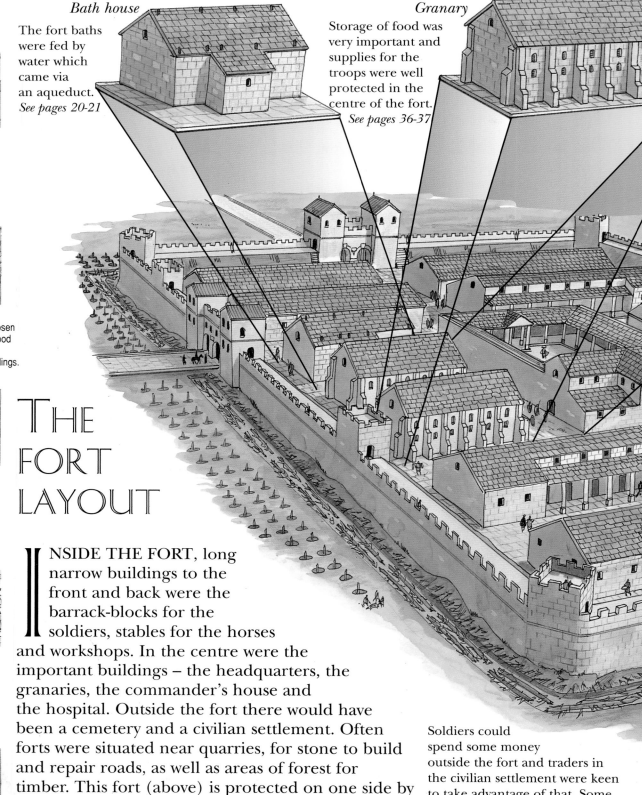

Bath house

The fort baths were fed by water which came via an aqueduct. *See pages 20-21*

Granary

Storage of food was very important and supplies for the troops were well protected in the centre of the fort. *See pages 36-37*

THE FORT LAYOUT

INSIDE THE FORT, long narrow buildings to the front and back were the barrack-blocks for the soldiers, stables for the horses and workshops. In the centre were the important buildings – the headquarters, the granaries, the commander's house and the hospital. Outside the fort there would have been a cemetery and a civilian settlement. Often forts were situated near quarries, for stone to build and repair roads, as well as areas of forest for timber. This fort (above) is protected on one side by the river and would have kept watch over the bridge that crosses it. Trees were cleared around forts so that anyone approaching could be clearly seen. The earth dug out of the ditches was piled inside the walls to strengthen them with a solid rampart.

Soldiers could spend some money outside the fort and traders in the civilian settlement were keen to take advantage of that. Some of the houses might have been homes for (unofficial) wives and children of soldiers in the fort. There was also a hotel in which official travellers and messengers could stay overnight.

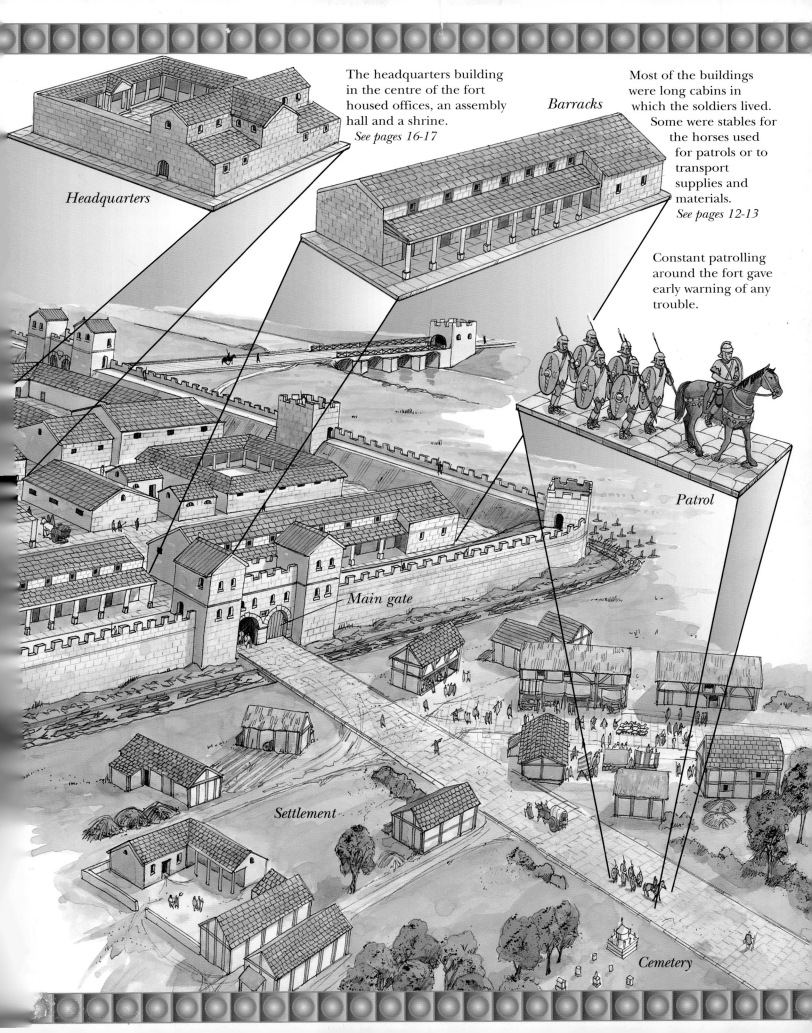

The headquarters building in the centre of the fort housed offices, an assembly hall and a shrine.
See pages 16-17

Headquarters

Barracks

Most of the buildings were long cabins in which the soldiers lived. Some were stables for the horses used for patrols or to transport supplies and materials.
See pages 12-13

Constant patrolling around the fort gave early warning of any trouble.

Patrol

Main gate

Settlement

Cemetery

THE BARRACKS

A FORT FOR A COHORT of around 500 soldiers would have had six barrack blocks, each containing the living-space for a century of 80 men. Plans that have been discovered show that barrack blocks were long and narrow, with the living quarters for the centurion in command at one end. In some parts of the Empire, barracks for the troops had two storeys. The barracks had foundations of stone and the upper parts had a framework of wood, filled in with rubble and plastered over. The building would have been roofed in tiles, stone slates, or wooden shingles, depending on what materials were available locally.

Centurions' helmets had distinctive crests. This meant they could be easily recognised by the men in a century.

The centurion had a suite of rooms to himself, including a separate bedroom and living room. Parts of his quarters may have been used as offices or storerooms.

The living quarters for the troops were cramped, with 8 men in two small rooms. One was used for sleeping, the other for their equipment, some of which took up a lot of space.

Auxiliary soldiers' quarters

Centurion's quarters

Barrack block

An auxiliary soldier's uniform was not 'standard issue', but the first item put on over the undergarments was usually a woollen tunic.

Over the tunic, chain mail might have been worn to protect the upper arms and body. This could reach as far as the knees and was heavy!

Troops wore leather sandals on their feet, their soles reinforced with iron studs. In colder climates, soldiers wore chunky woollen socks.

There were several different designs of helmet, but they normally protected against sword cuts on the cheeks and the neck.

Shields had different patterns for different units and were oval or rectangular.

13

FORT COMMANDER'S HOUSE

THE FORT COMMANDER lived in grand style, close to the centre of the fort and normally next to the headquarters building. Commanders' families often accompanied them on military service and every commander would also bring servants with him, as well as his own soldiers, to carry out domestic tasks. This house (right) has a central open courtyard with a series of rooms opening off it and is divided into three areas. A single-storeyed section with a main entrance contained the stables, rooms for the male and female servants, the kitchen and a small toilet. In the far corner were the main living quarters. The dining room and family living rooms were on the ground floor, with bedrooms upstairs. In colder parts of the Empire, the downstairs rooms had under-floor hypocaust heating (see p. 21). The third section housed a small private bath suite for the commander and his family.

The commander would have had his meals at his house. Servants baked bread in the small oven and there were supplies of meat, vegetables, dried foods and oil to the fort. The commander might also have brought in additional delicacies, such as Italian wine, not available to the troops.

The dining room was laid out in traditional style (below). A low table in the middle of the room was surrounded on three sides by couches on which the diners lay rather than sat.

Dining room

A DINNER PARTY

The dining room was cleaned and well-prepared for an important visitor such as a provincial governor.

The guests, commanders of nearby forts and their wives, began to arrive.

As soon as they had been greeted, the guests washed their hands before eating.

The first course was served: oysters were brought from the coast and served with other seafood.

Servants set out the dishes for each course. The diners took their seats, in strict order of rank, at the table.

The best wines came from Italy and were concentrated, so they had to be diluted with water before being drunk.

Venison for the main course. The deer may have been killed by the commander himself in the local forest.

A commander always had a supply of fresh horses available in the stables (below) in case he needed to go somewhere quickly.

The main bedroom was a private room into which the commander and his wife could retreat. No Roman woman in her position went anywhere without a number of female servants.

Main bedroom

Stables

At Rome dinner parties, guests made themselves sick between courses to make room for more food! On the frontier, the meals were more modest.

Local fruits, together with delicacies like figs and grapes brought specially from other areas were served for dessert.

The governor would have stayed in the commander's house, but other guests might have slept at the hotel in the settlement.

The servants had to clear up in time for an early breakfast.

Bath suite

The private bath suite was for the use of the commander, his family and invited guests.

If the headquarters had its own water supply, water could be drawn from the well in a shady corner of the courtyard.

One of the rooms off the courtyard was used to lock up soldiers who had committed crimes and awaited a judgement from the commander.

Supplies of spare weapons, armour, spears and swords were kept under lock and key, as well as bolts for firing from the ballista guns.

Troops were paid only three or four times a year. Part of their pay was taken for food, uniforms, weapons and tents.

On special occasions, all the troops assembled to swear their loyalty to the Emperor and the gods.

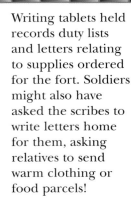

Seal for records

Writing tablet

Writing tablets held records duty lists and letters relating to supplies ordered for the fort. Soldiers might also have asked the scribes to write letters home for them, asking relatives to send warm clothing or food parcels!

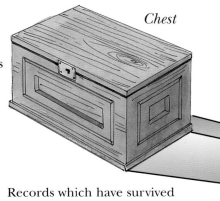

Chest

Records which have survived show that much of a soldier's pay was kept by the unit to pay for equipment, weapons, his uniform and his food. Payments were also taken for the soldier's retirement fund and for the burial club, which would make sure he was properly buried if killed in service.

Scribe

THE HEADQUARTERS

AT THE CENTRE of the fort lay the headquarters building. Inside the entrance was a large paved courtyard, often with a well in one corner, surrounded by rooms and a verandah. At the far end of the building there was a large hall with a high roof. Opening off this was a shrine containing the standards belonging to the unit of troops in the fort and sometimes also an underground strongroom in which valuables were kept. Rooms to each side of the shrine were probably used as offices.

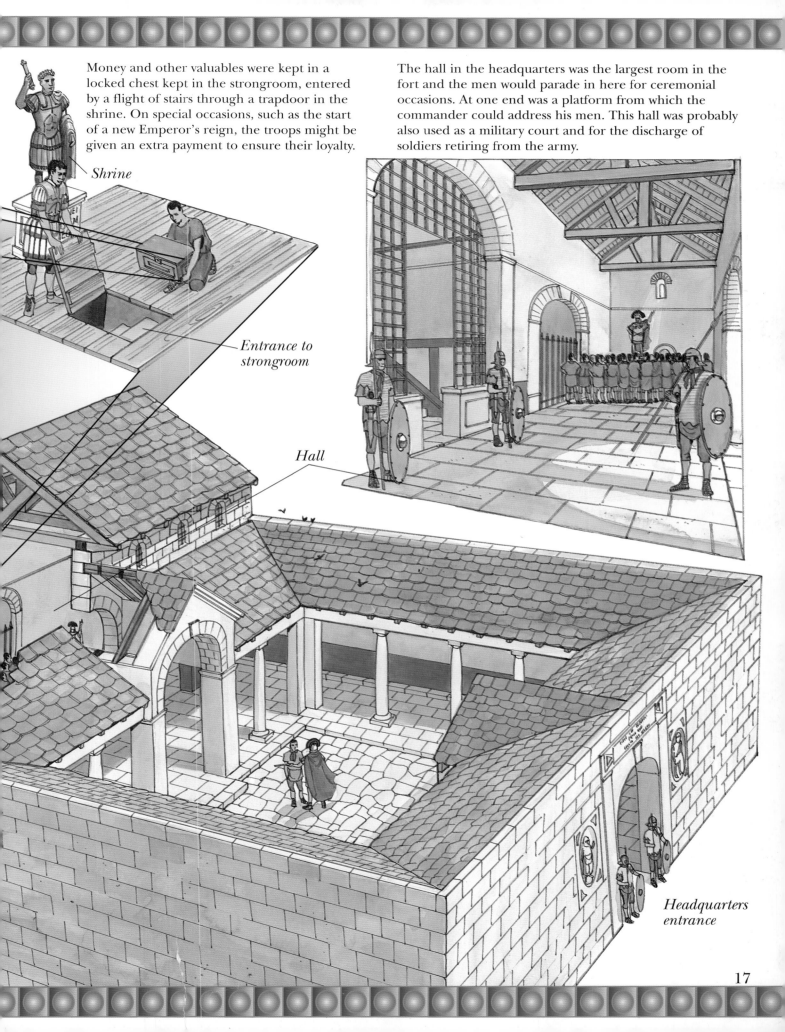

Money and other valuables were kept in a locked chest kept in the strongroom, entered by a flight of stairs through a trapdoor in the shrine. On special occasions, such as the start of a new Emperor's reign, the troops might be given an extra payment to ensure their loyalty.

The hall in the headquarters was the largest room in the fort and the men would parade in here for ceremonial occasions. At one end was a platform from which the commander could address his men. This hall was probably also used as a military court and for the discharge of soldiers retiring from the army.

Shrine

Entrance to strongroom

Hall

Headquarters entrance

There were four main gates, all of the same design and flanked by protecting towers. A stone inscription was often placed above the main gate, recording when the fort was built or had been last repaired. There might also be sculptures of protective gods – Victory and Hercules are shown on this stone found at a fort in Britain (right). Access to the fort was heavily guarded and one of the gates was often found walled up – if it was not needed it could pose a security risk.

Main gates

NVMINIB
AVGVSTOR
COHI IIGAL
F Q
TEC

Stone inscription

Ballistae could launch deadly steel-tipped bolts 300-400 metres

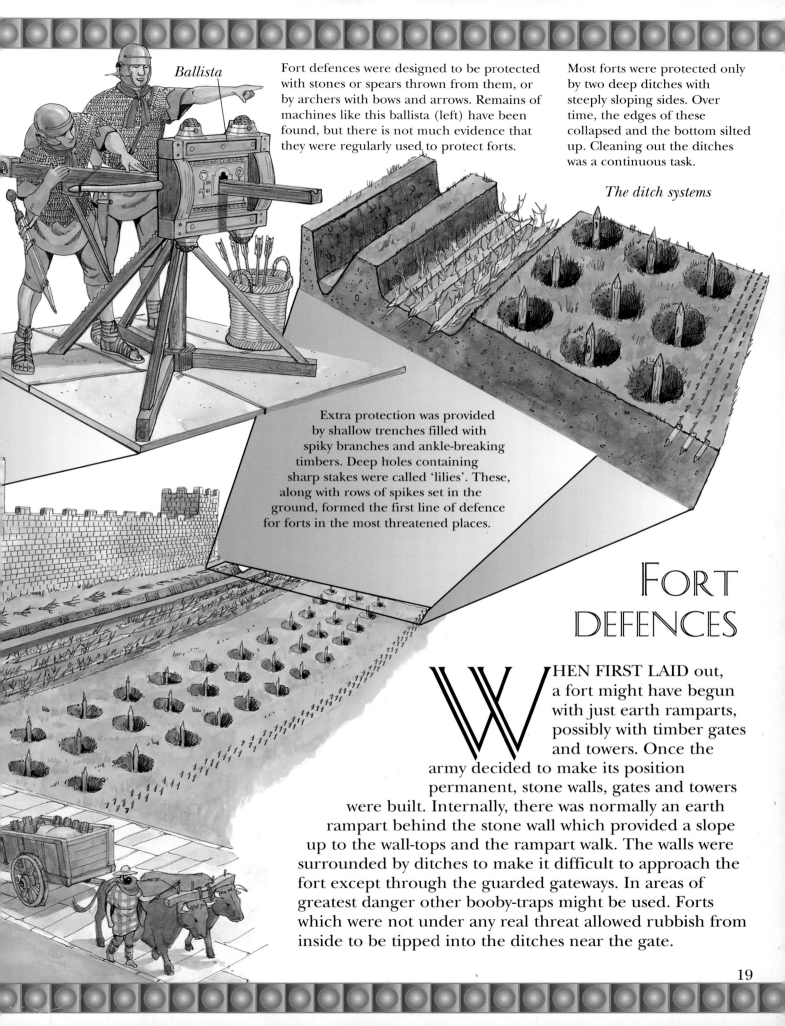

Ballista

Fort defences were designed to be protected with stones or spears thrown from them, or by archers with bows and arrows. Remains of machines like this ballista (left) have been found, but there is not much evidence that they were regularly used to protect forts.

Most forts were protected only by two deep ditches with steeply sloping sides. Over time, the edges of these collapsed and the bottom silted up. Cleaning out the ditches was a continuous task.

The ditch systems

Extra protection was provided by shallow trenches filled with spiky branches and ankle-breaking timbers. Deep holes containing sharp stakes were called 'lilies'. These, along with rows of spikes set in the ground, formed the first line of defence for forts in the most threatened places.

FORT DEFENCES

WHEN FIRST LAID out, a fort might have begun with just earth ramparts, possibly with timber gates and towers. Once the army decided to make its position permanent, stone walls, gates and towers were built. Internally, there was normally an earth rampart behind the stone wall which provided a slope up to the wall-tops and the rampart walk. The walls were surrounded by ditches to make it difficult to approach the fort except through the guarded gateways. In areas of greatest danger other booby-traps might be used. Forts which were not under any real threat allowed rubbish from inside to be tipped into the ditches near the gate.

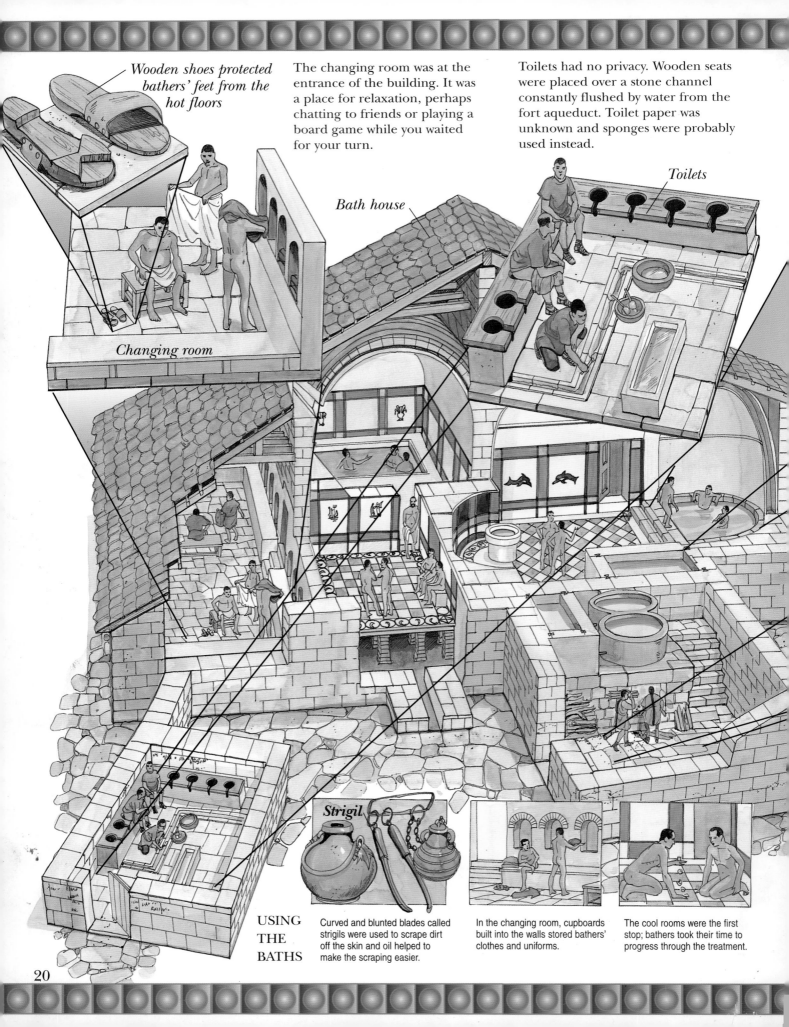

Wooden shoes protected bathers' feet from the hot floors

The changing room was at the entrance of the building. It was a place for relaxation, perhaps chatting to friends or playing a board game while you waited for your turn.

Toilets had no privacy. Wooden seats were placed over a stone channel constantly flushed by water from the fort aqueduct. Toilet paper was unknown and sponges were probably used instead.

Toilets

Bath house

Changing room

Strigil

USING
THE
BATHS

Curved and blunted blades called strigils were used to scrape dirt off the skin and oil helped to make the scraping easier.

In the changing room, cupboards built into the walls stored bathers' clothes and uniforms.

The cool rooms were the first stop; bathers took their time to progress through the treatment.

Warm bath (tepidarium)

After going through a series of rooms heated to increasingly warm temperatures, bathers eventually reached the hottest room of all in which water was thrown on the floor to provide a steamy atmosphere. Nearby was a warm bath (*tepidarium*) where bathers soaked for a time, before going back into the hot room again. Only after completing the treatment did they return to the cold bath (*frigidarium*) close to the entrance.

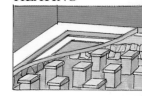

The bath house floors – and sometimes the living quarters of the commander's house – had underfloor heating systems.

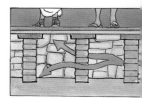

Warm air from the furnace was directed under the tiled floor which was supported by pillars of bricks. The floors could get very hot.

In the hottest rooms, the warm air also flowed through ducts in the lower part of the wall and came into the room itself.

The furnace was stoked by the troops on duty. They probably needed to use the bath house themselves after their work!

RELAXATION AND HYGIENE

THE BATHS were essential for the comfort of the troops. Soldiers kept clean by a combination of washing in large warm baths and by treatments in hot sweat rooms. After sweating, dirt could be removed by scraping their bodies with strigils – flat blunt blades. From the changing room, the bathers walked through a series of warm rooms, gradually increasing in heat, until cleansing had been completed. A plunge in colder water left bathers feeling completely refreshed. Crucial to the baths was a supply of fresh water and sufficient fuel to keep the furnace stoked to provide hot air for the underfloor heating systems.

Fuelling the furnace

The furnace had to be kept at high temperatures, since it had to heat up water in large metal boilers for the baths as well as keeping the hot air underfloor system supplied. Gathering fuel to keep the baths operating must have been a major task for the troops.

In the warm room, steam was produced from water splashed on the hot floor. It was heated by hot air circulating underneath.

The hottest room was closest to the furnace and was sometimes used for dry heat and sometimes steam treatment.

Thoroughly warmed up and sweating, the bathers used strigils and oil to scrape themselves down and remove dirt.

Bathers cooled off in the warm rooms, where it was also possible to have a massage.

A final plunge into a cold bath completed the treatment and left the bathers tingling!

THE MESS ROOMS

EIGHT MEN were supposed to share each pair of mess rooms but evidence suggests that many units operated with fewer soldiers than their full number. Even so, the two rooms must have been cramped and gloomy places to live. Small hearths have been found which suggest that soldiers cooked in their rooms and could keep themselves warm. In front of the fire there may have been room for a table and a bench or two where the soldiers ate and could play games – counters and boards have been found in several barrack blocks. The kit room had pegs, lockers and shelves to store clothing, armour, equipment and personal possessions. Quern-stones for grinding corn, cooking pots and drinking cups have often been found in this area of forts too.

Troops had to be up and ready before it was light. Armour was only worn for full duty.

As part of every meal, bread was baked in communal bakehouses in the fort ramparts. The loaves were round and flat.

Full equipment was worn when reporting for duty. The centurion inspected his men and gave out the tasks for the day.

Every soldier had to keep his own equipment clean and ready for use. Leather belts and scabbards needed to be kept soft. Swords and daggers were kept clean and sharp and bronze helmets were polished to look good on parade.

Auxiliary soldiers' sleeping and living area

Cleaning weapons and equipment

Patrol duties meant keeping a close eye on the countryside around the fort and watching for anything unusual.

Time off-duty gave a chance for slight relaxation. Weapons practice took place on the parade ground.

At the headquarters, news and announcements of job assignments were posted.

Swords and weapons were mended at the fort workshops, ready for collection.

The main meal of the day would have been something like bread with a stew of spiced lentils, onions and chunks of bacon.

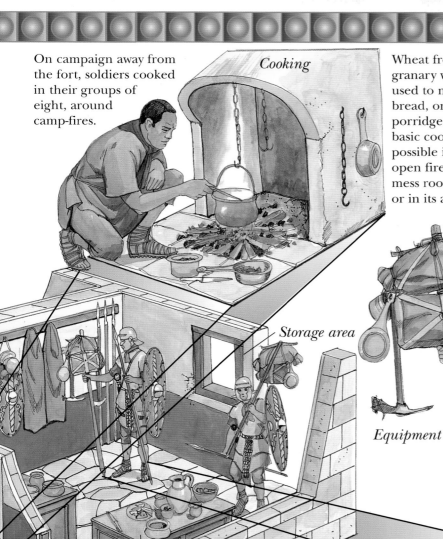

Cooking

On campaign away from the fort, soldiers cooked in their groups of eight, around camp-fires.

Wheat from the granary would be used to make bread, or a kind of porridge. Only basic cooking was possible in the open fire of the mess room hearth or in its ashes.

When on campaign, troops had to carry everything they might need with them. This included a leather holdall, a bronze dish for cooking, a flat bladed axe for digging and a turf-cutting tool. This was all attached to a long pole which could be slung over the shoulder.

Storage area

Equipment

At the end of the day soldiers returned to their mess room, unless they were on overnight duties. The centurion checked everyone in.

Soldiers had to return to the fort before the light faded.

Food

The basic diet of auxiliary soldiers was wheat, bacon, cheese and local vegetables, with sour wine or local beer to drink. This was supplemented with meat hunted locally, fish and other foods imported from further away.

Shopkeepers in the settlement would have sold local produce such as fruit and honey-cakes.

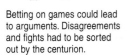

Betting on games could lead to arguments. Disagreements and fights had to be sorted out by the centurion.

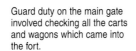

Guard duty on the main gate involved checking all the carts and wagons which came into the fort.

In their free time soldiers could go to the fort hospital to visit an injured colleague.

Letters could be written by the fort scribes. Soldiers sometimes wrote home to ask for warm winter underclothes to be sent.

In the evening it was possible to visit the inn in the settlement selling beer and local foods.

KEEPING A CLEAN FORT

A HUGE AMOUNT OF WORK was needed to keep a fort of 500 men running smoothly. Lists of soldiers' duties which survive show the types of tasks that soldiers had to do. The discipline imposed on the troops by their superiors was tough and some were well-known for their unpleasantness to their men. Punishments for disobedience or attempted desertion of the army could be severe. If men were caught running away they could be executed, though it was rare that a commander would insist on this.

Tending to the fort's animals was a major operation. Most sections of the army relied on horses, donkeys and mules to carry food, supplies and heavy equipment.

Duty lists that have been found show guard duty was an everyday task. The day was split into a number of periods to go on watch.

Centurions did not have to clean their own rooms or equipment – one of their troops did this and carried out the duties of a personal servant.

Settlement market places needed policing. There may have been disputes over short measures, theft or simple matters of law and order.

An extra pair of hands in the workshops to help the smiths repair wheels, axles or other parts of carts and wagons would have been appreciated!

It was a continuous job to keep the baths' furnaces going and stocked with wood.

Pitchfork

Specialist cleaners might be found in the fort settlement, but most soldiers had to wash their own underclothes and keep their bedding clean.
Only the centurion had a 'batman' to do it all for him.

Washing clothes and bedding

Rubbish disposal was always a problem. Sometimes a pit was dug at the foot of the rampart where kitchen refuse could be dumped. Rubbish was also carried outside the fort and dumped there. If it was not cleared, it attracted rats and other vermin.

Waste disposal

Cleaning the toilets must have been the worst duty and was also used as a punishment. It constantly needed doing, particularly if the water running through the toilets became blocked.

Cleaning the toilet block

ARMY DISCIPLINE

Centurions carried a staff of vine-wood, which they used occasionally! If you were guilty of a minor offence, you might be made to stand all day holding a pole!

Pay could be deducted if a unit had appeared cowardly in battle. Soldiers could be put on half pay for a year for serious offences.

A reduction in rank could be imposed on an officer who had deserted or mutinied.

Extra duties were imposed for more minor offences. These had to be done in addition to the normal range of duties.

In the most serious cases of desertion, mutiny or failing to obey orders, the punishment was execution.

25

PRACTICE MAKES PERFECT

THE ROMAN ARMY seems to have continually practised its drill. Parades on important occasions, for the review of all the troops, were particularly elaborate. Special armour for the men and horses involved in these events has been found at several places, including face-masks and helmets in gilded bronze.

In many places on the frontier of the Empire, temporary camps have been found – small rectangular forts built of earth and surrounded by a rampart and ditch. The space inside may have been where the troops pitched their tents for an overnight stay. Elsewhere, practice siege works have been identified, where the Roman army practised storming defended positions.

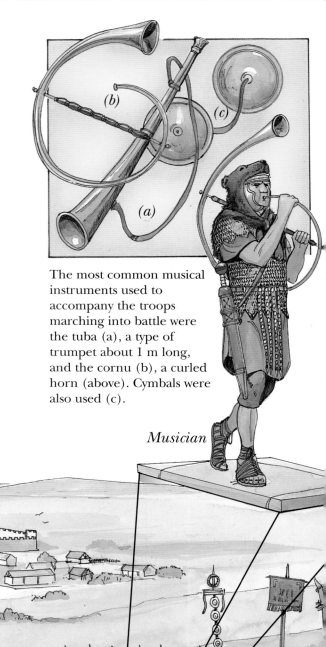

The most common musical instruments used to accompany the troops marching into battle were the tuba (a), a type of trumpet about 1 m long, and the cornu (b), a curled horn (above). Cymbals were also used (c).

Musician

Practising on the parade ground

The parade ground was also where the troops practised with wooden swords and protective armour. In readiness for battle the Roman army was well-disciplined and used its weapons effectively. The men protected each other and frightened their enemies.

Helmet

Parade mask

This mask (left) was not the sort worn by troops going into battle. The helmet would have been very costly and only used on ceremonial occasions.

The legate of the legion (right) based nearby reviewed the fort troops accompanied by his senior centurion.

Reviewing the troops

Legate

The standard bearer carried the unit's standards in front of a procession and into combat. Accompanied by musicians, the standards were held high to be seen by all the troops. The greatest disgrace for any unit was to have its standard captured.

Standard bearer

Senior centurion

The legate was appointed by the Emperor. To become a senior centurion a soldier would have fought in many battles and won awards for bravery.

Leather tents were enormously heavy and were held up by poles and ropes and pinned to the ground with wooden tent-pegs. Pictures of tents on Trajan's Column in Rome show that square sections of leather were sewn together to cover the large areas required.

Erecting a leather tent

If the unit was moving in hostile territory, more men were stationed to guard the ramparts and took turns at the night-watch. In most parts of the Empire it was unlikely that the Romans would face an army as well-equipped as themselves.

Keeping watch

ACTIVE SERVICE

O N CAMPAIGN into enemy territory, the army travelled on foot, each man carrying his own equipment. Once a site was selected for an overnight stop, a ditch was dug around the camp and the earth from the ditch piled up inside it to form a temporary defence. Guard was mounted to make sure that a surprise attack did not occur, but the key was to choose a site in the open, where enemies had no hiding place. More elaborate ditches were used to guard the entrances – the weakest points in camp defences. The troops slept in leather tents which were carried on baggage-wagons pulled by mules or horses. Each soldier shared an eight-man tent with the same men as in his mess room.

Camp layout

The layout of an overnight camp was the same as the permanent fort in which the troops lived. This meant everyone could find their way back to their tent in the dark, as each tent represented a mess room in the barrack blocks.

Leather tents became even heavier when wet and only the smallest could be carried by a single person.

Carrying a tent

The soldiers digging the ditch round the camp used the digging tools brought with them. They put the soil in wicker baskets and dumped it on the ramparts.

Digging a ditch

Ramparts

The earth from the ditch was banked up into ramparts. These gave a little more protection and allowed the soldiers to see further into the distance from a greater height.

THE FORT HOSPITAL

If a soldier was wounded and taken back to the fort, he was cared for in the hospital. In an auxiliary fort, this was a courtyard building with small wards, possibly including an operating theatre. Roman doctors were skilled at dressing wounds and removing missiles, as well as treating diseases of many kinds – a common problem among 500 men living together in cramped quarters.

Surgical instruments were used to deal with soldiers' wounds, including forceps for removing arrows from deep wounds, probes, spatulas and knives for operations. There were also tweezers and a glass beaker for putting ointment where it was needed.

Medical instruments

THE SETTLEMENT

OUTSIDE MOST FORTS lay a settlement of houses, shops, workshops and temples. Among these buildings was the hotel (*mansio*) in which official travellers, taking messages from fort to fort, could sleep overnight. Wherever the Roman army settled, the presence of soldiers with money to spend attracted traders offering goods and services of many kinds. Local industries selling clothes, leather goods, food or glass and metalware sprang up in many places. Although Roman soldiers were not officially allowed to marry while on active service, those who were permanently stationed in a garrison sometimes had unofficial wives and families living nearby.

Locally made pottery tended to be cooking pots and mixing bowls in grey or white, the shapes of which changed very little over many years. In some settlements, tiles for floors and roofs might also have been made.

Potter

The inn

The inn would have served a range of wine, depending on what was available – the best wine from Italy or Gaul or sour wine watered down to make it drinkable (just). The inn might also have provided bread and 'fast food' – perhaps a stew-pot of beans, chickpeas, pork or bacon.

Blacksmith

Blacksmiths provided a wide range of tools and implements for everyday use – everything from a pair of tweezers to a pickaxe. Bronze work was especially important, as decorated belt-buckles, pins and brooches were often made of it.

Leather skins and animal hides provided belts, straps, boots and sandals, as well as clothes, bags and holdalls. The army also used leather for sword belts, scabbards and tunics onto which metal armour could be sewn. Horse bridles and tents constantly needed repairing or replacing.

Leather worker/cobbler

Meat was difficult to keep fresh because there was no way of keeping it cool, so the fort's supply would have been local.

Butcher

RELIGION

Jupiter

IN THE ROMAN WORLD there were many gods and goddesses, ranging from those like Jupiter and Venus, who were part of traditional myths and stories, to the military ideals like 'Virtue' or 'Loyalty' which might be shown as goddesses. Many past emperors were also regarded as gods when they died. In addition to this, the city of Rome and her Empire was seen as a goddess. Taking the oath of loyalty to the army meant that soldiers believed in all these gods and promised to be obedient and committed to serving Rome. Troops also met local religions in their travels around the Empire such as the worship of the Persian god Mithras or the Egyptian gods.

Jupiter was the chief god in Roman heaven. Together with Hercules, he was often regarded as the protector of the army.

Discipline was one of the military virtues and was worshipped as the goddess Disciplina. Fort headquarters sometimes contained altars to her.

Disciplina

Mithras altar

The altars and a portrait of Mithras took pride of place in the temple, which was normally small and dark. The altars might have been used for incense or sacrifice and this one (left) would have been set up by a high ranking official.

DEOINV·M·
L·ANTONIVS
PROCVLVS
PRÆ·C·HBÁ
AÍONNAÆ
·V·S·L·M·

Hadrian's Wall carving

This carving (above), found on Hadrian's Wall, is thought to show Celtic gods. Brigantia, also found in northern Britain, was the goddess of a local tribe. This statue shows her in Roman style.

BRIGANAI SAMMDV
PESICCVJ·ÆATÍII

Brigantia

Mars was the god of war, going with the soldiers on campaign or into battle.

Mars

Temple of Mithras

Painting of Mithras

Mithras was a Persian god whose worship was popular among more senior officers in the army. Mithras himself was the god of light, who was born from a rock. He fought a wild bull, dragged it to a cave and killed it. The powers of darkness tried to stop the bull's blood reaching the ground, but the earth became fertile and bore crops. Mithras is often shown at the moment of killing the bull, surrounded by mystic signs and symbols.

Worshippers showed their devotion to Mithras by progressing through various grades of seniority. One of the grades was that of the raven (below).

Two attendants waited on Mithras, one representing darkness, holding his torch downwards, the other representing light, with his torch pointing upwards.

Attendant

The raven

The first Roman emperor, Augustus, was made into a god by the Roman people when he died. Emperors past and present were all worshipped by the army.

Bacchus was the god of wine and was often shown enjoying a party. He encouraged the exact opposite of Virtue and Discipline!

Even local beliefs, such as in the goddess of a local spring, might have led the fort commander to put up an altar to her.

Eastern cults were regarded with suspicion by officers. They encouraged soldiers in non-Roman behaviour, lessening their loyalty to Rome and its emperors.

Christianity only became widespread in the Roman army after about AD 300.

FREE TIME

Mock contests between soldiers dressed up as gladiators sharpened up combat skills and entertained spectators.

Wild boars, deer, hares and various birds would have been hunted around the fort and formed a useful addition to the troops' diet.

Mimes and comedy were popular throughout the Roman world and visiting players may well have entertained soldiers.

At festival times, everyone let their hair down. At the festival of Saturn it was the custom for servants to mimic their masters.

After visiting the inn, soldiers would be expected back in the fort in good time to be up for early morning duties.

Dice, made of bone or stone, have been found on many Roman fort sites. They were very similar to dice used today.

Dice

A daily workout might have included some friendly wrestling between colleagues, followed by a trip to the baths to clean up and relax!

Wrestling

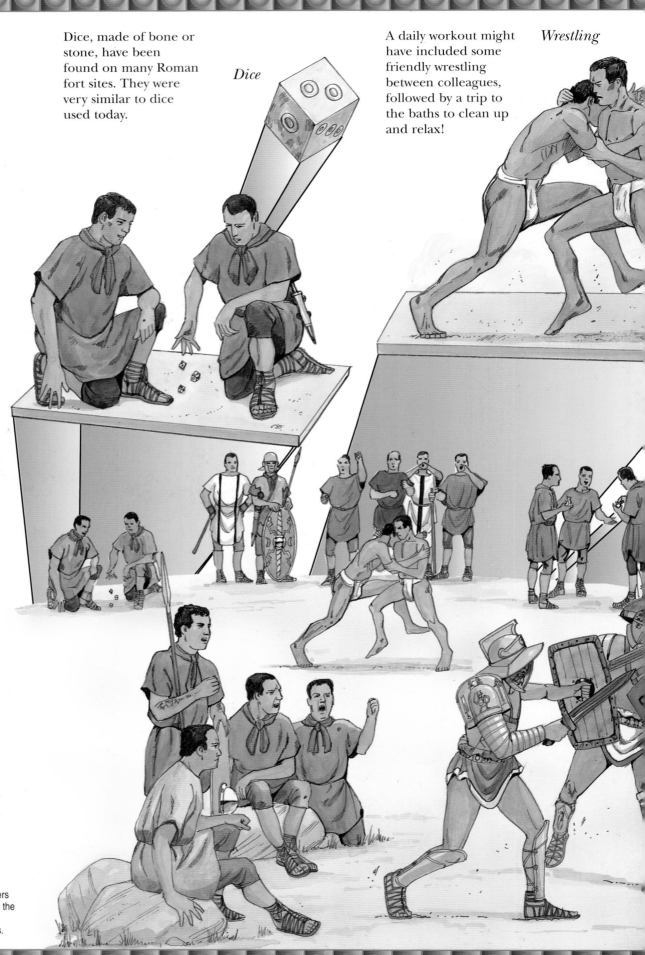

Gambling on the results of chariot races or fights between gladiators was popular throughout the Empire. No doubt soldiers found similar contests within the confines of the fort on which to bet their pay.

Gaming boards of stone like these (right) have been found in several Roman forts. Counters were made of stone, bone, glass or filed down pieces of broken pottery.

Gaming boards

A popular game, played on a board like draughts, was the so-called 'robbers' game' – the *ludus latrunculorum*.

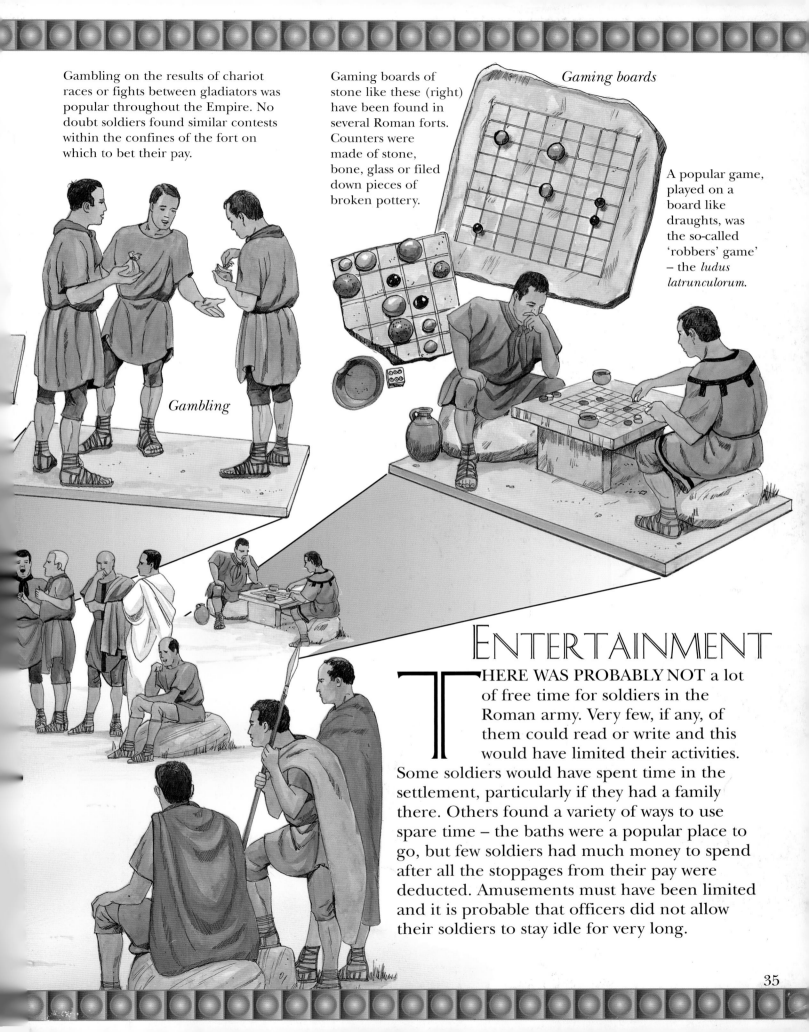

Gambling

ENTERTAINMENT

THERE WAS PROBABLY NOT a lot of free time for soldiers in the Roman army. Very few, if any, of them could read or write and this would have limited their activities. Some soldiers would have spent time in the settlement, particularly if they had a family there. Others found a variety of ways to use spare time – the baths were a popular place to go, but few soldiers had much money to spend after all the stoppages from their pay were deducted. Amusements must have been limited and it is probable that officers did not allow their soldiers to stay idle for very long.

THE GRANARIES

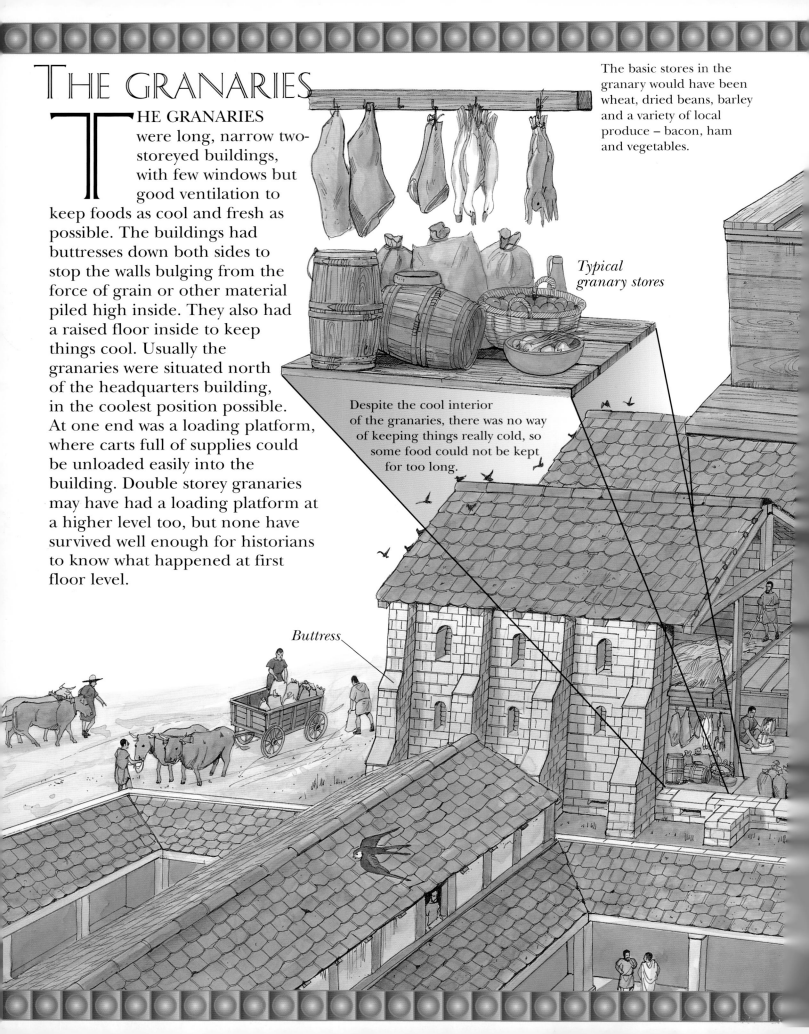

THE GRANARIES were long, narrow two-storeyed buildings, with few windows but good ventilation to keep foods as cool and fresh as possible. The buildings had buttresses down both sides to stop the walls bulging from the force of grain or other material piled high inside. They also had a raised floor inside to keep things cool. Usually the granaries were situated north of the headquarters building, in the coolest position possible. At one end was a loading platform, where carts full of supplies could be unloaded easily into the building. Double storey granaries may have had a loading platform at a higher level too, but none have survived well enough for historians to know what happened at first floor level.

The basic stores in the granary would have been wheat, dried beans, barley and a variety of local produce – bacon, ham and vegetables.

Typical granary stores

Despite the cool interior of the granaries, there was no way of keeping things really cold, so some food could not be kept for too long.

Buttress

Grain may have been stored in sacks or large wooden bins like this (below). It is possible that fodder for the animals in the fort was also kept in the granaries – it might have stayed edible a little longer if properly stored.

Storage bin

Bakehouse

FOOD FOR THE TROOPS

Wheat to make bread or to thicken meal or porridge was issued to the troops every day. The loaves produced were flat and round and probably quite hard!

Bread

Ventilation

Wines were transported around the Empire in large flasks called amphorae. They often had pointed ends to be sunk into the ground to keep their contents cool.

A thick fish sauce, known as garum, was produced in Spain and parts of Africa. It was transported in larger, round amphorae.

Olive oil and olives were very popular. The oil was used throughout the Empire for cooking and was stored in pottery flasks.

The troops made use of the goods available locally, such as oysters. Bacon kept longer when salted and cured.

Narrow slits in the lower levels of stonework allowed cool air to circulate under the floor. The raised floor also made it more difficult for rats or other vermin to get into the main part of the granary, where goods were kept. Insect pests were a nuisance and if they were not controlled, the whole contents of the granary could be lost.

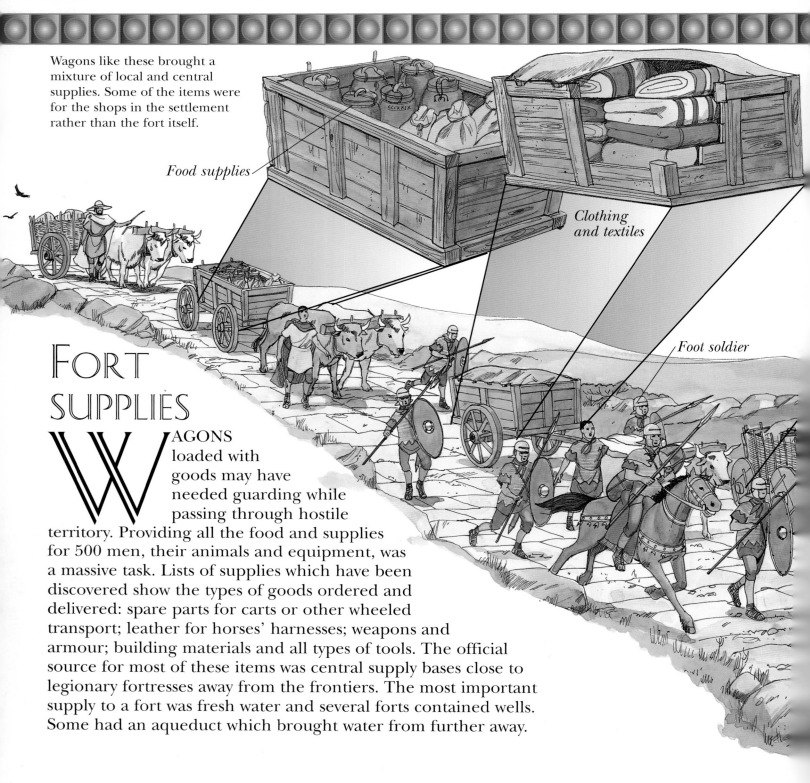

Wagons like these brought a mixture of local and central supplies. Some of the items were for the shops in the settlement rather than the fort itself.

Food supplies

Clothing and textiles

Foot soldier

FORT SUPPLIES

WAGONS loaded with goods may have needed guarding while passing through hostile territory. Providing all the food and supplies for 500 men, their animals and equipment, was a massive task. Lists of supplies which have been discovered show the types of goods ordered and delivered: spare parts for carts or other wheeled transport; leather for horses' harnesses; weapons and armour; building materials and all types of tools. The official source for most of these items was central supply bases close to legionary fortresses away from the frontiers. The most important supply to a fort was fresh water and several forts contained wells. Some had an aqueduct which brought water from further away.

BRINGING IN WATER

Engineers had to find a suitable place on a nearby stream where they could divert a flow of water downhill to the fort.

Soldiers dug a narrow ditch along which the water would flow when diverted from the stream.

As it approached the fort, the aqueduct normally came in close to one of the gates, where it could be supervised.

Inside the fort gate, there was a large tank into which the water flowed and from which a number of pipes led off around the fort.

Clothing and textiles were perhaps made in the area and brought to traders in the settlement. British-made cloaks were famous throughout the Empire because they kept the cold out so well!

Civilians who lived near a fort had to pay taxes to Rome. These might have been in the form of food or supplies for the local troops. It was hard luck if there was not enough left for the civilians themselves to eat.

The chances of attack against a supply column like this were remote, but it was always wise to stay on guard. A small detachment of foot soldiers and cavalry would have protected slow-moving convoys from being ambushed.

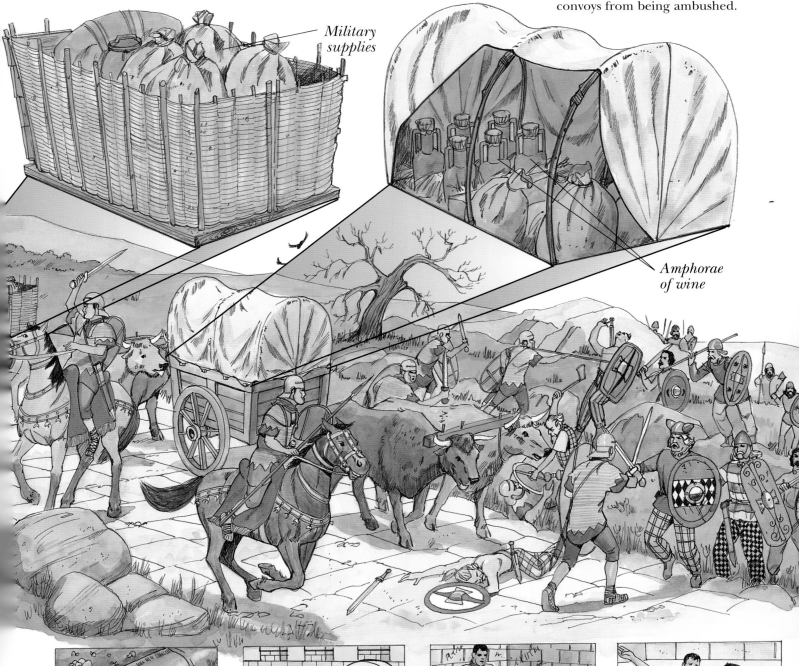

Military supplies

Amphorae of wine

Underground pipes of lead, tile or wood took water around the fort, using the natural contours of the ground to help it flow.

A series of tanks on the ramparts collected water for the troops in the barracks to use for washing and cooking.

Water was diverted to the toilets and flowed constantly through to keep them flushed. They still became blocked occasionally and needed cleaning out!

Another pipe led to the baths which used a lot of water – in the cold plunge, in the toilets and in the hot water tanks.

DISCHARGE FROM MILITARY SERVICE

While on active service, Roman soldiers were not allowed to marry, but once discharged they could have an official wife.

Former colleagues probably lived nearby, to remember past campaigns and triumphs with.

Many soldiers did not live long enough to complete their 25 years service – some were killed in action, others were struck by disease.

A discharged soldier's children became Roman citizens, with all their rights, privileges and duties.

One of the most important things a Roman citizen could do was to leave his land and property to his children when he died.

AFTER 25 YEARS' service in the army, a Roman soldier could leave with an honourable discharge. His service to Rome was over. At this point, an auxiliary soldier became a Roman citizen and received either a small pension or some land on which to live and set up house for the rest of his life. Quite often soldiers chose to live near the fort in which they had served, to stay near former comrades, to live with their wife and children if they had any and help the settlement round the fort continue to flourish. A retired soldier skilled in a particular trade, like metalwork or carpentry, might set up a workshop in the settlement and add to his earnings that way.

The unofficial wives and children of Roman soldiers often lived near the fort. When their father was discharged from the army, a soldier's children were also granted Roman citizenship, although their 'wife' was not. They could then get officially married, of course.

Formal discharge from the army probably took place in the headquarters, when the fort commander or other high official presented the soldier with a discharge certificate. This was proof that he had retired from the army and was a citizen of Rome.

Discharge ceremony

Unofficial wife and children

Discharge certificate

The discharge certificate was a bronze tablet which recorded the date of issue and the grant of citizenship – which included the right to marry – to the soldier and his children. Often there was a list of troop units in which all men who received the honour had served. The certificates acted as a kind of long-service medal.

After retirement at 45, soldiers might not have died for another 20 years.

A funeral procession to the cemetery would have been attended by family, ex-colleagues and men from the fort.

From around AD 125 bodies were cremated before being buried, so the procession went first to the funeral pyre.

Ashes were placed in an urn and buried in a small grave in the cemetery.

The burial club in the fort paid for a tombstone. It recorded the soldier's life and career in the army.

41

TIMESPAN

The earliest settlement at the site of Rome was a series of Iron Age huts, probably dating to the 8th century BC. For many years this settlement grew under the control of Etruscan kings, who controlled the area further north. Historians refer to two dates when discussing the beginnings of the city of Rome: 753 BC – the supposed foundation date of the city; and 509 BC, when the Etruscan kings were expelled.

All city states had to be able to defend themselves and Rome's early army was raised from the able-bodied men in the city. They were formed into units and companies based on the extent of their wealth – the richer they were, the more military service was required. Despite some serious defeats of this citizen army, Rome gradually became more powerful than its neighbours. This enabled the Romans to have what became a permanent paid army, something few other cities could afford.

509-260 BC By 500 BC, Rome was the capital of a small group of allied towns and states in central Italy. Over the next 250 years or so, this group was expanded through alliances, conquests and the establishment of Roman colonies. These colonies were often made up of retired soldiers and their families, who were granted land to farm and live on. By 260 BC, Rome was

beginning to dominate the whole of Italy and was brought into contact with other powerful states in the Mediterranean area.

260-146 BC The most powerful opposition to Rome's growth was Carthage on the African coast (in modern day Tunisia). After three major wars, including an attempted invasion of Rome by the Carthaginian general Hannibal and his elephants, Rome defeated Carthage. They gained five overseas provinces – Sicily, Corsica, Sardinia, Spain and Tunisia. By 146 BC, Rome's armies had pushed into Greece and Asia Minor (modern Turkey) and conquered these areas too.

Roman warship based on a Carthaginian design

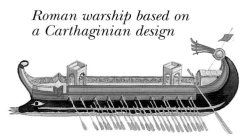

146-27 BC Further successful conquests meant virtually the whole of the Mediterranean coastline was under the control of the Romans. Some areas, such as Egypt, remained as independent kingdoms with loyalty to Rome. Rome's armies had by now become very powerful and their commanders could grow strong in their individual provinces. Some of them became a threat to Rome itself and the people's government

there. The most famous of these, Julius Caesar, used his position and fame from his conquest of Gaul (France) to have himself declared sole ruler of this vast territory. However, he was assassinated by men who believed that Rome should not have a single powerful ruler. It was left to Augustus, named by Caesar as his successor, to seize political power and establish himself as emperor.

27 BC-AD 14 The reign of Emperor Augustus established the Roman Empire. Thirty legions were now stationed all over the Roman provinces. Soldiers were still campaigning beyond Rome's borders, particularly in Germany, where the loss in AD 9 of three legions caused only a temporary halt in the expansion of the Empire.

Emperor Augustus

AD 14-69 After Augustus's death, the Empire was ruled by his descendants, some of whom had no military experience. Despite this, Rome's armies, under capable generals, were active in Africa between AD 17-24, entered Britain in AD 43 and increased their territory in Germany.

AD 69-96 The last of Augustus's descendants, Nero, was murdered in AD 69. After an internal war in which three other emperors were installed and quickly removed, an army commander from the east, Vespasian, became emperor. A year later, a long-standing revolt in Judaea (Israel) was crushed and Jerusalem was captured. The frontier along the river Danube in Germany was strengthened, the Roman army pushed into Scotland and battles began in Dacia (modern Romania).

Soldier's parade mask

AD 96-138 The greatest extent of Rome's Empire occurred during the reigns of Trajan (AD 96-117) and Hadrian (AD 117-138). During this period, the German frontiers were extended and Dacia was added to the empire after Trajan's conquests in AD 105. In the same year, conquests in Scotland seem to have been abandoned. By the reign of Emperor Hadrian, permanent frontiers were beginning to mark the extent of Rome's Empire – the building of Hadrian's Wall in northern Britain was started about AD 122.

AD 138-193 A relatively peaceful period, but with occasional serious campaigns fought against warring tribes, such as the Marcomanni in the Balkans area about AD 167. Scotland was reoccupied by the Romans between AD 143-163.

Triumphal arch in Rome

AD 193-211 Severe unrest began in a number of areas, with rival emperors emerging to threaten the stability of the Empire. Control was re-established by Septimius Severus, but his strength and power was not maintained by his successors.

AD 211-284 A time of great turmoil for the Empire. External threats were mounted and wave after wave of invaders – from many different directions – began to attack the borders. Between AD 235 and 270 there were 15 different emperors and for a time (AD 260–275) Gaul, Britain and Spain were under completely separate rule, with a different emperor to the rest of the Empire. Defence of the borders became critical.

AD 284-305 Order was restored by a strong new emperor, Diocletian, who reformed the army and split the Empire into two separate parts. West and east were ruled by a pair of joint emperors, each helped by a junior colleague. New command posts were created in the army with mobile forces who could fight wars, deal with invasions and supplement the more static frontier troops and their forts.

AD 305-337 Diocletian's arrangements for power-sharing broke down and by AD 312 there was a single ruler once again, Emperor Constantine. Reorganisation of the army continued and more powerfully protected frontier forts were built. Existing forts were modified to bring them up to date.

Christian symbol

AD 337-406 The Roman Empire became Christian following Constantine's conversion in AD 313. After his death, the Empire continued to be under siege from outside tribes. Frontier defences were continually reinforced and many battles were fought against invading tribes in Germany and the east. By the beginning of the 5th century, many of the frontiers were being overrun.

GLOSSARY

Altar A table on which sacrifices were made. Roman altars often bore a Latin inscription to show who set them up.

Amphorae Large pottery containers in which foods like wine, oil, olives and sauces were transported and stored.

Auxiliary Roman army troops or units, originally formed from non-Romans, which were added to the legionary forces.

Ballista An arrow or bolt-shooting machine, like a large crossbow, which used twisted ropes to provide the elastic power to shoot missiles.

Batman An attendant for an officer in the army who carries out all the officer's everyday cleaning tasks and is his personal servant.

Bolts Short wooden darts, tipped with steel, fired from ballistae.

Burial club A regular contribution, taken from a Roman soldier's pay, towards his burial expenses if he died while in service.

Buttresses Supports built onto the outside of a wall to prevent it from falling outwards.

Centurion The officer in charge of a century of men in either a legion or an auxiliary unit.

Century A division of men in the Roman army, normally 80 strong, commanded by a centurion.

Cohort A unit of around 500 men in the Roman army. A normal auxiliary cohort of infantry would contain 6 centuries, but some double-strength cohorts, with up to 1,000 men, have been recorded and could have been mixed infantry and cavalry.

Cult A formal way of worshipping the gods.

Desertion Leaving one's duty or failing to carry it out.

Dolabra The Latin name for the broad bladed axe with which Roman soldiers dug ditches and formed earth ramparts.

Drill Formal marching or other practice formations of soldiers.

Emblem A mascot or lucky symbol, adopted by a unit of troops and put on their standards or shields.

Garum A thick and concentrated fish sauce, made from fish caught in the Mediterranean and exported widely round the Roman Empire.

Gaul The Roman name for the area now occupied by France, Belgium, Luxembourg and parts of The Netherlands and Germany.

Groma An instrument (two cross-pieces mounted on top of a pole) used by Roman surveyors to measure straight lines and corners.

Hadrian's Wall A wall partly of stone and partly of stacked turf, built about 122-125 AD. It stretched from the River Tyne near Newcastle, England, 120 km to the west coast near Carlisle. Together with forts, towers and gateways, it formed a frontier barrier through which all traffic to and from Scotland had to pass.

Hypocaust heating A system in which hot air was circulated under floors to heat the rooms or baths above.

Legate The commander of a legion. A very senior officer in the army who might also have been the governor of the province.

Legion One of approximately 30 units of men, recruited from Roman citizens, who were the best trained and most feared soldiers in the Roman Empire.

Mansio A hotel in a fort settlement in which official messengers and those working for the Emperor could stay.

Official messengers People who carried official information round the Roman Empire, such as letters and instructions from the emperor or the governor of the province.

Quern-stones Rough round stones used to grind corn into flour for making bread. The bottom one was flat and the top one had a turning-handle and a hole down the middle.

Scabbard The sheath into which a sword is placed for protection when not being used.

Shingles Wooden tiles used as a roof covering, often cut from bark and used bark uppermost, so that rainwater runs off.

Shrine A holy place where gods are worshipped.

Trajan's column A 38-m high column in the forum at Rome. It was built by Emperor Trajan between AD 107-113. The marble column is covered with carvings telling the story of the successful wars in Dacia (Romania). They show many aspects of the Roman army in action.

Verandah A covered passage down one side of a building, open on one side and held up by columns.

Writing tablets Slim leaves of wood covered in a thin layer of wax.

INDEX Page numbers in bold refer to illustrations

A
amphorae 37, **39**
animals 24, 37
aqueduct 10, 20, 38-39
archers 8, 19
armour 9, 16, 22, 26-27, 38
army, Roman 6, 8-9, 42-43
auxiliary soldiers 8, **8**, 9, 13

B
bakehouse 22, **37**
ballistae 16, 18-19, **18-19**
barracks 10, 11, **11**, 12-13, **12-13**, 22-23, 28
bath house 10, **10**, 20-21, **20-21**, 24, 34, 35, 39
baths, commander's 14, **15**
batman 24, 25, 44
blacksmith 31, **31**
burial 41, **41**
butcher 31, **31**
buttresses 36, **36**

C
camps, temporary 26, 28, **28**, 29
cavalry 8, 39
cemetery 10, **11**, 41
centurions 8-9, **8-9**, 12-13, **13**, 22-23, 24, 25, **27**
children, soldiers' 10, 40-41
cleaning the fort 24-25, **24-25**
clothing **8-9**, 13, **13**, **38**, 39
commander's house 10, 14-15, **14-15**
cooking 9, 14-15, 22, 23, **23**, 37, 39

D
defences 18-19, **18-19**
desertion 24-25, 44
dinner party, commander's 14-15
discharge from army 17, 40-41, **40-41**
discipline 24-25
ditches 19, **19**, 22-23, 24, 26, 28, **29**
dolabra 9, **9**, 44
drill 26
duties 24-25

E
emperors, Roman 6, 16, 17, 27, 32, 33, **33**, 42, **42**, 43
entertainment 34-35, **34-35**
equipment 8-9, **8-9**, 13, **13**, 22-23, **23**, 28, 31, 38

F
festivals 34
food 10, 14-15, **14-15**, 16, 22, **23**, 30-31, 36-37, **36-37**, 38-39
fort layout 10-11, **10-11**, 28
frontiers 6, 15, 26, 43
furnaces 21, **21**, 24

G
gambling 23, 35
games 20, 22, 34-35, **35**
garum 37, 44
gates **11**, 18, **18**, 23, 24
gladius 9, **9**
gods 16, 18, 32-33, **32-33**
granaries 10, **10**, 23, 36-37, **36-37**
groma 10, 44

H
Hadrian's Wall 6, 9, 32, 43
headquarters building 10, 11, **11**, 14, 16-17, **16-17**, 22, 32, 36, 40, **41**
hospital 10, 23, 29, **29**
hotel (*mansio*) 10, 15, 30, 44
hunting 14, 34

I
inn 23, 30, **30**, 34

K
kitchens 14, **14**

L
leather worker 31, **31**
legate 27, **27**
legionary soldiers 8, 9, **9**, 27

M
medical instruments 29, **29**
mess rooms 22-23, **22-23**, 28
musical instruments 26, **26**

O
official messengers 10, 44

P
parade ground 26
patrol duty 11, **11**, 22, 28
pay, soldier's 16, 25, 35
pottery making 30, **30**
practice 26-27, **26-27**
punishments 24-25

Q
quern-stones 22, 44

R
ramparts 10, 19, 25, 26, 28-29, **29**
relaxation 21-22
religion 32-33
records, military 16, **16**
recruits 6, 8
Rome 6-7, **6-7**, 28, 32, 39, 40, 42
rubbish disposal 19, 25, **25**

S
sandals 13, **13**, 31
scribes 16, **16**, 23
settlement, civilian 10, **11**, 23, 24, 25, 30-31, **30-31**, 35, 38-39, 40
shields 8-9, **8-9**, 13, **13**
shingles 12, 44
shrines 11, 16, **17**
stables 10, 11, 14, **14**
standards 8-9, **8-9**, 16, 27, **27**
strigils 20, **20**, 21
strongroom 16, 17
supplies 8, 11, 14, 16, 36, 38-39
swords **8**, 9, **9**, 13, 22, 26

T
taxes 39
temples 30, **32-33**
tents 16, 26, 28-29, **28-29**
toilets 14, 20, **20**, 25, **39**
traders 10, 30
training 8, **8**
Trajan's Column 28
tribes 6, 43

V
verandah 16, 44

W
wagons 8, **8**, 23, 24, 28, 38, **38-39**
water supply 10, 12, 16, 21, 38-39, **38-39**
weapons 8-9, **8-9**, 16, **16**, 22, 38
wine 14, 23, 30, 37
wives, soldiers' 10, 30, 40, **40**
workshops 10, 22, 24, 30, 40
writing tablets 16, **16**, 44

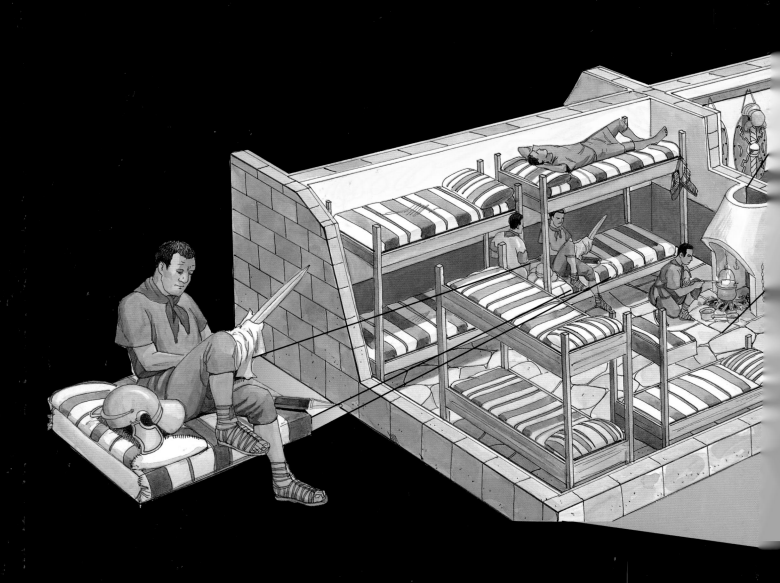